Flood Plain

Flood Plain

Lisa Sewell

Grid Books BOSTON

GRID BOOKS
Boston, Massachusetts
grid-books.org

Printed by Sheridan
Grand Rapids, Michigan

ISBN: 978-1-946830-32-6

CONTENTS

Dedicated to the memory of:

Shirley Sewell Rothschild

1927–2022

Phillip Rothschild

1952–2022

Edith Phillips Sewell

1926–2023

The tree is no impression, no play of my imagination,
no value depending on my mood; but it is bodied over
against me and has to do with me, as I with it—
only in a different way.

Martin Buber

Art is continually haunted by the animal.

Gilles Deleuze

A Visitor

White Salmon, WA

A ruby-throated soul among sparrows
smaller than them and lighter,

who returned on the shadowy rim
of December to hover at the blue

glass feeder—dipping a feathered tongue
into the empty wells, then buzzing away

to snatch a spider from its web—
all the black-chinned Rufous

and Calliope kin in Baja by now
or the Caribbean, where hurricanes

are finally through unmaking houses
and unmade daughters and sons

still wait for relief. But with the fires
done too and the AQI finally green,

even someone like me could step outside
for a short walk and return

from tindered fields to find him,
hovering, breath white among sparrows

sliding the air right up to my face
like a spirit messenger, not mine

but someone's—the thin
metallic song whining in the dusk.

One: Waterways

Mean Season

Oxnard, CA

The *Santa Anas* of my childhood
are back, red katabatic winds

that make your hair stand
electric, that begin as a cold mass

and warm as they unroll and surge
through the Santa Monica range

where the Woolsey fire has jumped
the 101 and is heading for the coast.

They rustle the hibiscus and palm trees,
the unevenly trimmed hedge

of cherry laurel as a stranger stands
on his balcony, shading the air around his head

with smoke. Joan Didion said those winds
dry the hills and nerves to flash point and likewise

suddenly the man is gone: I watch him slide
between the sliding doors and emerge

street level, frantically swiveling his head east
then west then east again before breaking

into a run like a person pursued
or possessed by an invisible charge.

In this beachfront neighborhood
we are praying the winds don't shift,

that the air remains invisible.
The neighbor at 5238 Surfrider

fires up his blowtorch. Brief sparks jump
around his hands and helmeted face

and everything holds its breath
until the buzzing stops. Now the stranger

returns (he wasn't out for a jog)
with a red heeler named Antoinette.

He speaks to her in clipped
censuring French: *saloperie, putain de merde*

over and over as if his own unsettled soul
were lurking there, trying to escape.

Incilius periglenes (golden toad)

Because his screech is melody
and we are all in jeopardy

and all have golden toad songs
semaphoring in our throats;

because the golden toad teaches us
to flirt with explosive day-glo

breeding excess and to only emerge
between the dry and the wet;

because the true toad occurs
on every continent

except Antarctica and Australia
and is toothless, deaf,

and mute, and all the scientists
admit their gold protective skins

that were also lung
and kidney were like nothing

anyone had ever seen
or will ever see again,

we must memorize the numbers
of decline: from three hundred

or more in each small pond,
to twelve the next year,

then one lone male
in 1989, for in the end

all his flaxen chorusing
could not conjure a darker

gravid female to climb,
clutch and hang upon.

Now, we cannot conjugate
them in the present tense

or in the understory and gnarled
roots of elfin forests

and cannot return
with our notebooks and quadrats

to that April–May window
and temporary pool, to the small,

bright, gold-enameled
orange shapes that occasionally

called out, perfectly patient,
perfectly still. Nothing

to record but the end
of a wild dangerous ride

like the second plague
from Revelations in reverse

or the frog-in-the-moon eclipsed
back into oblivion by a black,

human magic. Too late to regret
the fungus and blight ushered

across oceans and mixed
with the dirt beneath our fingernails,

or wipe away the dust coating the Vibram-
soled hiking boots of the new conquistadors.

Swimming Pool

North Hollywood, CA

All summer my mother swam laps, lifting her head to touch the edge, breathing on one side, crossing back and forth over two hundred times to swim a mile, and you couldn't interrupt her.

*

When I fly over my old neighborhood and leave California behind, luminescent turquoise kidney shapes, ovals, and parallelograms dot the grid. When I was growing up, even working-class families like mine on the east side of the train tracks had pools.

*

Home movies are watery and blue: Zuma Beach, the wading pool from Talouca Lake, the built-in pool on Ethel Avenue, my father teaching my sister to dive like a racer—to keep her back straight, to push off from the edge with toes and fingers, hands over head to skim the surface.

*

We dove down to touch the green sea horses in the deep end, played Marco Polo, bump butts, competed to see who could make the biggest cannonball or do a backflip off the edge, who could hold their breath the longest swimming the breaststroke under water like skinny frogs, skimming the pale blue bottom with our fingers.

*

You wore a cap to keep the chlorine from ruining your hair and your hair from ruining the pool's filter, but even with goggles your eyes burned.

*

In one movie, my mother lies on the chaise lounge in her two-piece, raising her hand to shield her eyes, telling my dad to *stop, stop*. She too seems to be underwater, unable to make her words heard.

My grandmother floats in the shallow end trying not to get her hair wet, smoking a cigarette.

*

Chlorine sensitivity may cause skin redness, tenderness, or itching. In some cases, rash, crusting, or hives can develop. Others suffer from nasal congestion, runny nose, or sneezing. In those with asthma, it may trigger wheezing and shortness of breath.

*

The earthquake lifted the water up like a tidal wave and flooded the front part of the yard, sinking between the red bricks of the walkways, bleaching the crab grass. We heard that a neighbor who always swam in the early morning was thrown onto the concrete beside the pool. He broke his shoulder and several ribs.

*

At Sima's Swim School we learned the crawl, the breaststroke and backstroke, to dogpaddle and float. On the first day, as instructed, I put my face in the bleach-tinged water and blew bubbles. Both hands on the edge in the shallow end, legs extended, I learned to kick.

*

My mother liked to show off her girlish figure and always swam in an impractical two-piece. My favorite was purple with delicate green stripes that she had sewn herself. She never learned to breathe on both sides. Or to do a flip-turn.

*

Easter vacation in Las Vegas, we stayed at the Executive Suites instead of the Thunderbird or Circus-Circus. Each set of little bungalows had its own private pool and there were only a few families to share with. My sister must have been old enough to swim because she was supposed to be watching me as I drifted on the shiny green inflatable into the deep end and slipped off.

If I fell in, if I sank to the bottom, if the water closed over my head, how could I have seen the sliding glass door of our suite slide open and my father come dashing out in his royal blue Speedo bathing suit?

*

Fall and spring, Christmas and summer, I fly from Pennsylvania to California to help out with my mom who mostly sees shadows now and whose words have sunk into a weedy swamp. Her needs, winnowed down to meals, showers, sleep, the bathroom.

The last time, at night, I heard her voice through the thin bedroom wall, crying *no* or *stop* or *go away* from the mossy core of our nightmares.

*

I swam through a difficult year in a pool designed by Bernard Maybeck and Julia Morgan. Surrounded by marble columns and statuary, in the middle lane, I synchronized my distance from the fluttering feet in front of me, practiced my flip turn and got my mile down to thirty-two minutes. I repeated the poems I had learned by heart, *One must have a mind of winter, There is a certain slant of light*, matching the stroke-stroke-breathe of my crawl to a hymnal beat until the day I got out and couldn't make it to the locker room. I lay down on one of the narrow benches that lined the walls, exhausted, like I had taken a sleeping pill that wanted to pull me under.

My doctor said I'd developed an allergy to chlorine.

*

On one flight back to Philadelphia, a wild thunderstorm over the airport prevented us from landing for at least an hour. When the turbulence stopped, I stopped clutching the arm rest and pressed my forehead hard against the seat back. I held my own hands tight, and tears slid down my chin to my neck. I wasn't afraid of dying and I don't pray, but I prayed the violent listing and buffeting would not start up again as the plane circled the airport. *Please*, I whispered. I just wanted my body back, to remain in my seat—not shoved, not lifted or sliding against the vinyl, my stomach settled, not dropping down or pushed against my throat.

*

In May, we helped my father move the sandbags and pull the plastic cover off: algae lined the sides, fist-sized frogs with pale green backs and limbs akimbo floated on the surface.

All Day

after Allen Ginsberg and for the men in English 4615

All day (& a night) the men carry
their howls inside & are carried

through corridors of no & no invention,
of pat down & strip search,

death march & death imagining. All day
they are inside & unsafe, coming of age

between high walls & high water, breathing in
the prison-numbered air & breathing out

fantastic, nearly fatal susurrations & pleas:
howls that are the rations they keep,

always under guard & always hailed
having been those *best minds* & having borne

all indignations, free & unfree & more inside
in barred rooms that I will never see.

*

In barred rooms that I will never see
& passageways behind sliding metal doors,

they stand for count four times each day,
are herded (& hurt) from maximum block

to laundry or shop, from ding-wing
to dining hall. In the hole or the hospital

for observation, in the library & chapel
they keep the shades drawn & keep me

in their prayers even when they believe
a woman like me has no reason to care

about injustice, pray my mother
keeps breathing the free air, that I return

to them repaired with my books & papers
to our windowless white-boarded classroom.

*

Here, in the windowless white-boarded room,
in the education wing, our twenty-five chairs

circle the empty space of conversation. I hold
their pages close to my face as they read & nod

uh huh, *oh yeah*, & I think *I'm with you*, Eddie & Akeel,
Terrell & Hakeem. I'm with you Lawrence

though you are seasick & landlocked
behind your DOC-issued glasses

in your regulation browns. I'm with you
in your clauses & rhymes, breathing in your lists

of prisons built on landfills & toxic
garbage dumps, tasting your holding cells

& cages. Rafael's arm is on my desk, almost
touching mine as the white shirt stands guard.

*

As the white shirt stands guard, I'm learning
the syntax of systematic processing,

of flatweeding & random checks, of sixty-plus
on J-block against all regulations. I'm with you

in the yard with *dope boys & stick-up kids*,
& in the daily dread of *graveyard life*

& *walking dead.* I'm with you as you *pass
those dead-man flyers without blinking,*

trying to learn the holy news of leaky bodies
staying human—blind to indignations

you keep off limits & off the page, painting an inside
that might protect me from the non-life

& sorrowing I drive away from
with nothing but my wishes.

Trichechus manatus (manatee)

In small eyes that recede in grief
apology, or indifference,
in their entanglements,

we find a baffling resemblance—
their moving flippers moving
toward the hungry mouth to feed.

Just for us they demonstrate
a lazy home-grown entertainment:
barrel rolls and body surfing grace,

the utility of doing nothing
but grazing all day, interrupted only
by three or four trips to the surface

for long lung and body full
yogic breathing. The only mammals
to evolve back from land to pond

some fifty million years ago,
they know the small furry hyrax
in their genes and like the elephant,

in their pachyostotic bones they remember
Stellar's sea cow, hunted to extinction
in only twenty-seven years.

They wear the scars of their collisions.
It's how we recognize and know them
as they loll and roll, beat the food

into their mouths and grind their molars down
with grinding. They turn their whole
bodies to watch the pleasure swimmers

float illegally into view. The crocodiles
may occasionally disturb them
in their pretty shallow bays and estuaries

but their only predators are humans.
Stellar noted that during a hunt when one
was cut, all the others were intent on rescuing

and keeping it from being pulled ashore,
though scientists are certain
there is nothing social in their aggregates

or signature moans, nothing but hunger
in the squeals and chirps. Some say they forget
that humans cannot breathe in water

or sing in tune with the music
of the Morae. Some say they drown us
out of spite, that you must bind yourself

hand and foot or be bewitched
by the gentle calm that casts a spell
on every man who passes.

At Glen Canyon National Recreation Area

Page, AZ

We come to see up close
the concrete ramp and famous

one-hundred-and-ten-foot bathtub ring,
desiccated dregs the color of fiasco and cash-

register dreams, to roll our kayaks
in the clear warm broth of nostalgia

and glide in the shadow of the seventy-story
concrete plug: the Colorado River

Storage Project (CRSP) engineered
to aid the reclamation of arid

and semi-arid lands, to light up Phoenix
and Las Vegas and even parts of LA

where I stayed up late in childhood
burning electricity, and to girder

a cow town called Page into
a multi-million-dollar industry

and level out the flow—drowning
a wild river in a reservoir

breaking the *extremely unstable*
irascible body that can roar

through the canyon in a gigantic flood
or fall back after the melt

and trickle quietly, unproductively
all summer long.

*

At 2 a.m., three days ago, the doctor
called to say *your ninety-year-old mother*

has presented to the ER in extremis
with sepsis and no advance directive,

do you want us to administer antibiotics
and fluids? Behind the dam

sand rises by increments every week,
making the waters of the Colorado

silt-free and crystalline, the same way
the vancomycin clears up the infection,

scouring the small intestine
killing friendly and unfriendly bacteria.

In the informational film from 1963
machines of heavy construction

and detonation bring new voices
to the land of the Navajo. The narrator says

the lake *is a man-made natural wonder,*
a meandering and warm companion

to the cold-water dam-controlled
waters of the Grand. *Drain Lake Powell?*

I don't think so, one commentator insists
over variations on the theme of "Wayfaring Stranger."

*

From the plane it dazzles, turquoise
and verbose, a branching curved

many-coved, multi-legged and -headed
arthropod or dragon, spreading wings

and pointing emptying fingers at the
desert business. *An intimacy. A jewel.*

With water levels almost at dead pool
canyon sites are re-emerging,

ghostly, shrouded in chalky brown-gray.
Floyd Dominy claimed they *didn't have to relocate*

anything—there was nothing there but artifacts,
like the sickle carved from mountain

sheep horn in Lizard Alcove, a bag
of cotton seeds, a yucca-leaf sandal

and jar of salt left in Benchmark Cave
beside the ash ring from a fire

for roasting Yucca hearts in springtime—
a saygee bowl (late Pueblo) still stained

from a meal left unfinished
when the unnamed and unknowable Anasazi

were interrupted by calamity or worn down
by drought. *Oak set glens, fern-*

decked alcoves, mounded billows of orange
sandstone. One hundred and twenty-five

side canyons, each one different, each one
with a look and a voice and a feeling of its own.

*

It's a half-hour paddle to cross Wahweap Bay
to Antelope Island's drowned coves

and sandless shore. Though no one
wants to see or touch the sludge-

stained bottom, and no one is permitted
to touch the body of a first love

turned contagious, quarantined and undone
by medicine in fevered writhing

in a hospital room three hundred miles away,
I put my bare hand against the face,

coating my fingertips in drought,
silt staining my fingers like an aftertaste.

That night before I go to sleep
in my orange tent, surrounded by RVs

I check my phone and find an email
from the home health aide—

the *C-diff* is back, just like I expected,
feverishly colonizing and competing

with healthy intestinal flora. For now,
I rest my cheek against the grave

Navajo sandstone, furrowed by crinoid
fragments and vertebral smears, and a deeper

indentation where some Mesozoic reptile
scraped along the muddy bottom as it swam.

Rigging Day

Lee's Ferry, AZ

It's difficult to see
where a mother lives
after the foreseeable fall,
the narrowing of arteries—

and to know she lives
inside those thickening walls
and narrowing arteries.
Impossible too, to know what grows

inside the thick aortic walls
of confusion and blindness
to fathom the *C. Difficile* growing inside
with unpronounceable names

wreaking blind confusion.
And when fever spikes severe
it feeds on unspeakable names
like *toxin*, *colitis*. You know

that kind of fever, spiking and severe,
her body, an incubator
of toxins, colitis,
of vomiting and inflammation.

With her body like an incubator
wracked and changed
by vomiting and inflammation
and roiling unholy pains

she's on the rack and changed:
nothing is a given anymore
but roiling, unholy pains,
rivering pollution and dissent

that gives nothing anymore
but flailing leukocytes and platelets.
A river of pollution and dissent
laps against all her shores

with its leukocytes, anemic platelets,
long after the foreseeable fall
the collapse of all her shores,
unquiet, unruled and difficult to see.

Phantom Ranch

Grand Canyon National Park, AZ

A gleam, a flash that's gone
before it's spied—not sun
but shimmer of black tail, black wing
or some precious thing snatched in a flash
and a gleam that's gone before it's spied
being carted toward a secret beach
or rocky crag down canyon. Sooty and noisy,
a passerine, a songbird, at every stop
a pair of ravens surveyed our camp, eyeing
your camera, demonstrating skill
with zippers and diversion until a gleam
so flash was gone before we spied
my yellow scarf aloft, a minor sun,
and your watch swift and glinting in raven flight:
fodder for the mess of sticks, fur, bark
and hair, the four to seven eggs dyed
the same uncanny turquoise green
of Havasu Creek and the Little Colorado.

Field Notes on the Toroweap Formation

Prospect Canyon, AZ

Sixteen days undertaken to take in and to be taken
    on the water feed of daily releases from the cold

underbottom of Glen Canyon dam. On the sixth day
    of our trip, the seventy-third of John Welsey Powell's

second journey, I said good-bye to the Coconino shale,
    good-bye to Mauv limestone, having unpacked and repacked

my tackle and tools. Powell came to solve the mysteries
    of four-hundred and fifty miles of river through desert canyons,

and found hundreds of sites to survey,
    name, and define, erasing everything that was there

with his imagination: Marble Canyon, Flaming
    Gorge, Horseshoe Bend, Redwall Cavern. Powell's notes,

at first full and even fulsome, dwindled as the situation of the party
    became constantly more desperate, and at last became mere jottings.

*

Underway and under sway we came for the wilderness
    that was never wild, for vast distances never empty,

to walk the narrows of Blacktail canyon and span
    a billion years with a fingertip pressed to the Great

Unconformity where recently formed Tapeats sandstone
    rubs against the ancient Vishnu Schist. We found

our *great unknown,* but with every eddy mapped and every current
    quarantined between two reservoirs that fill with silt

and lose a foot of storage each year. It was difficult to sleep
    and in the mornings I woke to half-light, lying crossways

on the raft, adrift or beached by shifting, regulated tides,
    everyone else asleep and dreaming of the hike to Deer Creek,

everyone except the yellow-shirted man banging beer cans
    into disks—filling his dry bag with our collective excess.

*

Trip lengths vary depending on propulsion. We were not
    motorized. We faced the worst headwinds in twenty years

for June someone said. Everyone irritable and exhausted
    by noon, by 1 p.m. My John was not the trip leader

and could not be blamed for missed campsites and side canyons,
    for the coffee and potatoes at the bottom of Bedrock Rapid,

but he suffered the missed eddies and broken oars
    of near-calamity. His arms and back and abs and legs

the engine that drove the raft through Hance and Granite
    and Crystal. Mostly, I wasn't there to witness, gliding instead

through the needle's eye in my kayak, skimming the edges
    of hydraulics the eighteen-foot raft could punch right through,

though sometimes I was buffeted by currents, grabbed
      by the throat (at least that's how it feels) and pulled asunder.

*

The afternoon headwinds were fierce and even
      with vertical drops, from the shore I watched John

stalled and silhouetted, windstruck and standing still,
      trying to slam the oars forward with his hands.

Imagine lining the wooden boats over most of the broken water
      with ropes. Or after half a day of hard labor, feeling the rope,

then the boat pull, then bounce, spin out and tumble down Unkar
      or Lava, supplies, and coffee mugs, plates and flour

spilling, spreading and floating downstream, something
      always broken that cannot be repaired, an oar or desire,

the skin on your hands. Exhausted beyond measure, sunburnt
      and sandwhipped, John was asleep by 8 p.m. or even 7.

*

I kept company with his dreams which were vivid
      and made him scream or cry out, *fuck you you fucks,*

or *help me no help* in a voice that arrived from the bottom
      of a well. I sang a secret sweetness into his nightmares

and when I slept, dreamed the milky blue of Havasu Creek, the moon
      at its core and the ghostly humpback chub

where sweet waters meet the chilly measured arms
     of the main. It's the only place those chub survive

     and in the early morning light I could not sleep through,
I tilted my page to catch the glow, to rend the broken lines

     and broken waters, to chapter through the days
but *brought back only scraps of what the expedition taught*:

     names and profiles of ghosts, all the riverine shrubs,
bushes, trees and grasses that no longer thrive.

Current's End

Pearce Ferry, AZ

A skilled boatman has many routes
through, many lines to take and be taken on

but peak flows correspond to peak needs
in Phoenix where air conditioners run

on high half the year, as predictable
as seventeen years of drought.

If you go in May, in June, in August,
September, be prepared

for twenty-foot waves in Hermit, a Lava Falls
that earns its name. Past Travertine rapids

and Weeping Spring, past Bridge City
and Separation Canyon, you'll wake

at the finish line, sober on the final morning
of the final day, your rafts lashed together,

as you pass like ghosts through a wide
ghost canyon over phantom rapids submerged

by Lake Meade, water murky
with seventy years of silt. Even the Tamarisk,

invasive, an eyesore, cannot grow
on the shores of this man-made lake.

Dry for decades the sign at Hoover Dam
cheerfully explains. When I first saw

the photograph of the Colorado
where it reaches Needles, CA, I assumed

it was a painting: a metaphor of depletion
by an artist who had imagined the river's

pale blue expiration in the desert,
the milky waters dividing into paler webs,

petering out on hardscrabble oceans of sand.

Megaptera novaeangliae (humpback)

With no vocal cords to speak of, the males float head down
to intone the long complex soundings—densely patterned

with theme and repeat. Does he sing to intimidate or attract,
of fitness and challenge or the alluvial need to charge the other

and rise belly-to-belly out of the sea? Do the moans and shrieks
bring news of the long migration from ground to ground,

of memory's flensing deck and flensing knife, the cruel winch
and the aftermath on the long New Bedford beach: the carcasses

massing into the distance—though this is my memory
of a photograph in the Pilgrim Memorial and Museum in P-town

when I couldn't imagine what the dark beached mounds
could be or why the proud men stood aft and fore and starboard.

A female might breach thirty times or in a notion of sea-flight
and sea-gallop, silently flee (for only bulls can sing) from cove

and net toward the open—her car-sized heart running
full throttle, her slender goose-fleshed great New England

wings and blood ablaze, her young breathing air
in the elsewhere. Is she rising now, open-mouthed and feeding

through the bubble-netted krill, dividing the Atlantic
as tourists bend over the ferry rail to look long

into the whirlpool of swallowing? No one can stand
the spoiled fish stench or turn away from the churn

and spin of that briny downward cycle, with all the ordinary
muxin and skimshander of daily life laid aside,

amid the gurry water, oil, and sludge the cutting
leaves behind. But in a small wooden boat

directly over the vertical keener, in a quiet boat at sea,
you might hear the singing through the narrow hull and know

that what left her lungs rose later as a spout in the distance,
a loud shout or the briny sigh of long-nerved valor.

Line 901

Santa Barbara, CA

With the giant warmwater patch
nicknamed "the blob" fluorescing

in the Gulf of Alaska and off the coast
of California, and new weather patterns

failing to suck enough heat
from the oceans; with weird fish

on the beach and bright red, cooked
lobsters, brightly colored tuna crabs

washing up by the thousands at Dana Point,
on Refugio Beach and El Capitan, another

surprising visitation from the future arrived,
leaving forty-six rescued sea lions and twelve dolphins

cloaked in petroleum, three-hundred and ten
dead birds and mammals to collect and log.

It was an 11 a.m. story of corrosion,
one hundred and five thousand gallons

of heavy crude that had coursed through the Plains
All American pipeline 901 at steady flow conditions

darkening the sand and rocky shore, slicking
the ocean. The workers in Midland, Texas,

who turned off the alarm to address another issue
would be found not guilty. The corroded pipeline

would be purged, filled with an inert gas and closed
indefinitely. And those of us who were driving

and just in time to see the boats release their dispersant
and the crews begin their work, would find

windows up or down, there was nothing
we could do against the stench that waters eyes

and sears the nose and throat like the opposite
of air, an invisible veil of smoke, galloping through our lungs.

And later, those walking on beaches as far south
as San Diego would find that neither turpentine

nor mayonnaise could not wipe clear
the carrot-shaped islands of tar

on the calloused soles of their feet,
black stain beneath the pinky toe, indelible.

Chelonia mydas (green sea turtle)

Weather is not climate: a cold winter
means nothing to rising waters, sinking beach

to cold-blooded sapling beings,
blood warming with the oceans by degrees.

In *The Book of Ceremonies* the turtle
is one of the entities that possesses spirit—

and during the Tang Dynasty turtle shells
were used for divination. Some believe Chinese script

was derived from the markings on their backs.
They cavorted with the dinosaurs

and when the searing vapor cloud rained hot dust,
along with the lizards and angiosperms,

they sailed across the K-T boundary
through millions of centuries to us.

*

Now all along the underwater sounding
lines they fly at speed: their shoulders

like rounded prows, their flippers wings
that conveyer them from the Galapagos

to Malaysia, from Ascension Island to Brazil—
for every turtle can navigate by the earth's

magnetic field. They float and dive, rise
and sink from sandy beach to islands

of sargassum where hatchlings feed
and breathe, endangered in the danger zone.

*

From science we learn the egg-tooth
that vanishes, the three-chambered ventricle,

the delicate calipash and calipee
tasting of empire and victory overseas.

Neither fish nor fowl, they chew grass
like cows, swim like seals and breathe

with lungs and through their skins,
absorbing everything. The flexible scutes

that pattern their backs only shatter
when the angel shark's teeth meet their mark

or when dropped from the winch
onto the purple riprap of the breakwater.

*

Columbus and his crew *saw tortoises
of a vast bigness and in such numbers*

they covered the sea, closing the gap
between ship and sand, as though

you could stroll across their backs to conquest.
Greenback, soup turtle, *tortuga blanca*—

once in the Caribbean, I too followed her
through hurricane-bleached reefs

as she swam through eel grass
and algal blooms that turn their fat buttery green.

It takes an hour for the mother to dig down
and unload one hundred or more

leathery eggs, then drag her body back
to the comfortable sea. She is long gone

when the shore turns as gothic as Violet Venerable
in *Suddenly, Last Summer*, with the desperate

midnight scramble and bird-dark sky
and *all of us trapped by this devouring creation*.

*

I think I learned from Lewis Carroll
that turtles weep, though not in agony

or grief. The sea turtle isn't sentimental.
She carries four elephants and the globe

on her back and only falters amid fish trawls
and plastic shopping bags. The shells used

to divine the future never foresaw
the petroleum we cannot live without,

or the eighty-seven days the broken deepwater well
billowed and gushed. But I must admit

that black currency into this reverie and remember
the two hundred miles of coastal seashore

oiled with turtles and birds
washing up from Port Arthur, Texas,

to Apalachicola Bay—in the longest unusual
mortality event recorded in the Northern Gulf.

Path of Totality

Lincoln City, OR

At the tsunami evacuation zone
where the river meets the ocean waves,
the harbor seals raised silvery heads
to watch me watch them in the dusk
that came that day near noon

just like they said: above us, in the sky
the iris blew, expanding to the diamond
engagement ring. The animals seemed calm,
but I was grateful when the nighthawks flew
and pigeons returned to roost, not on the Pacific coast

but somewhere. When you are in the sea,
not of it, you float or sink or dog paddle
mindless, entranced. I thought what it might
mean for an eclipse to arrive without science,
to try to run from the spectacle of God's

wrath believing this was it, like learning second-hand
the middle-aged caregiver I'd hired to live
in my mother's house, who once drove fifty miles
to LAX to pick me up, hid the phone,
and said terrible things to my mom

in the shower, like *fuck if I'm going*
to touch those nails and shouted
at the neighbors too. Though I was warned,
I never believed the ocean can lift
and then pound a body to the sand

with just the slightest swell, pulling all the precious
and semiprecious stones from my fingers
leaving me ringless. These hands
have been the overlord and harbored illusions
of fairness. Now they get what they deserve:

let them thrash uselessly here, stripped
in the dark at the end of the world.

Flyover Country

North Platte, NE

Then the stately waders point skyward

    and are gone. Night-flyers,

day-flyers, they flee the Gulf coast

    in clusters and threes

in early spring. Not silent, they point

    skyward, hundreds of thousands

winging hundreds of miles and more

    each day. They ink the sky

from edge to edge a dusky gray and darken

    the air with a trumpeting *karroo*,

converging on the Platte River Basin,

    to rest and fatten midway through the last

great North American migration.

    Ancient, resilient they too made it through

the End-Permian extinction, now

they refuel, roosting in the shallows,

testing the iron-rich ooze—the stain

on their plumage like a rusty kiss.

By April they're off again:

pointing skyward and night-flying all the way

to Alaska and Siberia on tawny wings

of supplication and praise.

Two: Estuary

Back to the Mat // spring tide // Estuary

You need a block and lots of patience to be
the open mind of a window cracked open,
a dusk-colored curtain, a silvering, a chime—
though everything is optional. With the tide reigning,
a cairn of rock and feathers to keep the fry
and fingerlings rearing in the estuary, I waited
in *tadasana* for clarity and judgment. I wanted
to begin again with a curious heart
even as construction of a thirty-foot wall
at the border began, for every fisherman knows
there are times the fish are biting and times you stand
in your waders stone cold, though I am not a fisherman
or a fisher of men. I have no soul, only skin
and a list of three hundred possible factors
to explain the *solunar activity* of fishes and tides
and the electric wave that uncoils my fingers and names
the boon companions I didn't know would find me:
sandpiper, common murre, bladderwrack.

Establishing a Base Line // 0.4 ft tide // Mitchell Marsh

With the oystercatchers and common murre,
the bladderwrack and pearly everlasting, I commit

to showing up every day with my mat—my intention
like a thread or steady flame that carries me away

from the invasive scotch broom and reed canary grass
that line the edges of the marsh, from news of unregulated

gas development in the Keystone state. I stand
where winter grasses lie supine on flood plain

and riverbed, both at once, where twice daily, waters pulled
by the moon pull back—and twice daily return

to drown and feed the salt-accepting sedge, everything blown
and blowing and courted by a wind so strong it too

must be factored in. Even on a clear day, here in Otis,
from a biplane or helicopter, you wouldn't see me,

one leg folded, arms stretched into *vrikshasana*,
but you'd see the way the blue-green tidal fingers curl

and meander, spelling out the inscrutable marshy heart
of the estuary, now beating strongly into my hands.

Creating Space // 6.1 ft tide // Cascade Head

Heart beating strongly, the wind at thirty knots
whips rain against the punky, gray-to-black

cliff ledge, the smashed green and amber beer bottle glass
among the thrift and the sea pink. It rifles

the trapped Safeway bags and buffets
the red-tailed hawk who regarded me too briefly

as I tried to witness self, to witness breath, thumbs
pressed to my chest in *anjali mudra*, beginning

to see that no single person or agency is in charge of
combatting foreign election interference.

On almost any long car ride anywhere in North America
almost anyone will spot the hawk's broad,

rounded wings and short, wide tail, his rufous belly
streaked with brown—the dark band of pulsation

between wrist and shoulder. I let my own arms dangle,
unclench my shoulder blades taking the fold

from the inside out and vibrate with the *kee-eeeee-arr*
screech as he telescopes to a wavy line and hovers—

there to receive what is there to be received,
as the fascia begins to tear and slowly open.

In the Moment // 5.5 ft tide // Estuary

I take what is there to be received, more rain, more sky
torn open to a hooring, a scow, a raff? In this light,

there is no language for no horizon, for sky and air, sand,
rock and river all degrees of gray, for the violent trembling

of arms and thighs as my stance widens or contracts. At 9:45,
when congress is voting to gut internet privacy, *solunar*

activity is three out of four fish strong and everyone
is here on the strand: the man in the fluorescent green-

and-black running suit who leashes his dog, the barnacle-
encrusted rocks—the Western grebe, winter visitor,

uncommon and peripheral, who dives down, then flies
or swims with wings back to the surface and reappears

with a bivalve in her bill. Is she dreaming of the courtship display—
the lunging-forward dance across the river, side by side

in perfect synchrony, bodies praised and upraised turning
the flashlight beam inside my mind into a floodlight.

Binds and Balances // -.5 ft tide // Estuary

In the flashlight beam of dusk, a bevy
or lodge of otters feeds, snouts up, jawing
small fish or razor clams into a pulp
that can be swallowed. One skitters hunch-
backed across the sand, one preens
the bright underfur that keeps her afloat,
chirping out strophes and iambs that skitter
along my spine and neck and buoy my hapless
arms and ungrasped finger bind—though far away
in corridors and waiting rooms the supreme court
is unraveling fifty years of my freedom.

The otters keep watch, alert each other, fish
for one another and themselves. But I read
about a family that bit and scratched
some summer teenagers who ran screaming
from the muddy waters of Lake Shasta
and can't help but wonder if these three
swim amiably beside the skin-divers
who hunt Dungeness crab in the brackish stream
and later peel off their wetsuits by the car.

I keep my gaze soft and my hands to myself
or pressed together in prayer to create
a circuit of energy as powerful as the otters'
dorsoventral undulation that raises
a silvery ridge on the river's murky face.

Heart Opener // 1 ft tide // Cascade Head

Far above the river's murky face, I slip past
the barbed wire to prairie grass and mud-narrowed trails

with the tuffaceous siltstone of an open heart.
I try to visit sensation and keep my eyes soft

notice the squirrel-made caches of hemlock seed cones
lining the hoofprints of Roosevelt elk, once hunted

on these slopes for their upper canines. Brown-black wool
scarves their necks as they unlock the understory,

masticating new leaf buds in the thicket
just beside the trail, their third and second stomachs

rumbling wildly, their storage stomachs filling up
with March. On my way up the hill, the young runners

leave it to me to move aside, to let them pass in their brightly
colored tights as the elk twitch and shift, rotating ears,

rearranging their herded positions when I startle
them with my sudden step and sharp

little intake of breath, opening my palms
to absorb the benefits of my practice as the EPA

rescinds the ban on chlorpyrifos, and noticing
how things have shifted in my practice so far.

Moving Meditation // neap tide // Experimental Forest

Things have shifted. I practice deeper and knock on the door
of the hibernating landscape, splattered with mixed
debris and browned withered fronds. The radiating spokes
of a rimless wheel pry my eyes open and I finally see
the fiddleheads disrobing along the trail and an aftermath:
tufts of ground squirrel gray-brown fur along the path.

Among the branches, April's rustle and slash of indigo,
Stellar's jay is on the hunt, coloring the air between
the branches. Habitual nest-robbers, compulsive liars,
they squawk in crow and robin, squirrel and cat and chainsaw.

But I want them to carry me too and do not hesitate to fill my feeder
with the seeds they love, as though I haven't learned a thing,
as though I don't believe they are cruel, and known to eviscerate
small warblers, like the red-breasted nuthatch or dark-eyed junco.

Finding the Center // low tide // Mitchell Marsh

Small warblers in steep decline
accompany me (red-breasted nuthatch,
dark-eyed junco) sending my heart forward
and my shoulder blades back. Today I choose
the ubiquitous Pacific wren to be my guide.

Round and brown, he hops amid the spikey chaos
of salmon berry, tail upright, body shaking
with what one ornithologist called
the pinnacle of song, though soon I am lost
again, careening in my bright blue
parka along the muddy edges of the field:

intention gone, shoulders burning. Up the coast
in Neskowin the Douglas firs buried in sand
and poking up into the surf zone were not petrified
or turned to stone. They retain their pithy
heartwood and inner bark, enduring berms
and iron dikes, and the shaking of never-
before-encountered muscles and thighs.

Like the scags lying on their sides and littering
this marshland, they are waiting for the earthquake
that will bury or release them, sealing the cycle.

Align and Stabilize // 0.8 ft tide // Crowley Creek

To seal the cycle, I must bury or release
the mind, rotate my palms and let the tailbone

uncurl as though US warships were not on their way
to the Korean peninsula. Here in Otis

green is greening and the varied thrush
resounds his reedy single note long enough

to fill the forty acres of old growth hemlock
and spruce he needs to thrive. Sorrel and miner's lettuce

carpet the ground and beside the creek, a row
of alder have lain down their branches

like an offering or plea. Seemingly flung
down by the wind they lunge away

from the bank, their white
lichened trunks prostrate in the grass.

Not broken nor ruined, their root nodules
are still fixing nitrogen and feeding

the soil, though the perfect ovoid leaves
on their branches have nowhere to grow but down.

Exploring the Edge // bore tide // Estuary

With nowhere to go but down, no leaves or branches
the harbor seals breathe and doze on the spit

where salt and fresh waters mingle. They slide
into the surf and vanish, borne upstream

by the tidal bore, trusting the body can be held
as if in a hammock, free of burden, free of weight.

I too must give myself over, forget the drone strikes
reported to have killed two hundred civilians

and notice instead the quiet rise and fall of my chest,
the spacious thoughts like waves. I keep watch

for the bowls of silver fur that break the surface, that disappear
and appear again a few feet closer, gravely raising shoulders

and sleek heads to regard me, raincoat shrouded, wavering
on the shore. Their coal eyes fill with what looks like reproach,

though it may be curiosity. Like Bishop says, it's clear
they are believers in total immersion. Named sea-dog in Dutch,

they will follow your kayak upstream and you must resist
the urge to plunge in or run a palm across their wild animal heads.

Whatever else the seal knows, for a moment in her gaze
I am on a rocky shore and I linger there to dissipate.

Giving in to Gravity // spring tide // Cascade Head

Fog lingers, dissipates, and clouds soften. I mingle gladly
with the thorny blackberry lining every inch and turn
along the steep pitch and switchback trails. I forget about Plath,
her bush of flies and ardor for the jubilant black summer fruit
to come. Everyone here works hard to keep the meddlesome brambles
from staking out new ground: the orange-vested high-schoolers
with shovels and shears, the winter herd of Roosevelt elk,
even the storm-clouded air seems to object, rushing beside
and behind the pair of bald eagles full-wing-spanned
above my head as I break open to the open field
without judgment or opinion, asking myself, *in the power
that vidabhadrasana gives, what's there for me?* Far below,
the seals bake slowly on the spit. Their supine, charcoal shapes,
like hash marks on a cell wall, counting off our days.

The Energy of Flight // ebb tide // Estuary

Like hash marks counting off our days,
the fern-like yarrow (little squirrel tail,

pretty carpenter, poor-man's slipper)
is stalked below, stalkless above, and suddenly

everywhere I step, toes struggling to lift
and separate, anchored by what I give

and get back, unlatching the hollowness
in my bones. Named for indestructible Achilles

and used to heal the wounds of soldiers
fallen in an ancient war, it is bitter on the fingers

and pungent in the steamy sickroom air,
a helpmeet and balm that restores the breath,

a common weed and common nuisance—
hunted and removed like the beavers

that swim unseen in the braided channels
of the estuary. Only the hydrologist

loves their precarious dams and webbed
hind feet, their rodent wisdom and tidal

expertise: she told us that in winter at king tide,
on the exact spot where we were standing

surrounded by reed grass, the waters
would close right over our heads.

Turning Off the Lights // 4.9 ft tide // Estuary

Over my head, the wind, a few gulls winnowing
the mist. I lie back, legs extending, open my mouth
wide and sigh, and sigh again, as the smirr taps
wet messages on the estuary floor. My back
against the sand, I give in: unlatch my shadow
that blackens and contracts with the short and darker
days. With every seventh wave the tidal bore
sends small breakers up the mouth of the delta,
carrying me deep into *shavasana* and for as long
as I want, the teacher says, I can take as much
time as I need. But if I am in charge and it's all up to me,
how can I receive the benefits of my practice or awaken
from this dead man's pose I have welcomed and mastered?

Progressing to Headstand // neap tide // Experimental Forest

Welcomed and mastered, the Great Blue
Heron flew from the bushes. I flushed it,

as they say. When it follows or leads us
down river in our boats, it feels like luck,

though all along its hollow bones
is the memory of ancestors hunted

for their size and a gray-blue
feathery flourish for women's hats.

Along and behind the green path,
the branches of Douglas fir

and Western hemlock are everywhere,
summer-furred, ornamental with nuances

of moss: slender mouse-tail, rough-stalked
feather, appellations that fill my mouth

as I stand toes splayed and lifted
into the impossible, feet unsteadied

by what I give and get back. But the mosses
do not falter. They thrive in the interstices

and have been with us from the start,
making soil, purifying H_2O, and rolling

all along the spine of the earth to massage
the lifeline of being. I call them bryophytes

and wonder how to live unfixed and between,
as if to unseal the cycle by bowing my head,

and pressing my thumbs once again
against my sternum though everything is optional.

Three: Plains

Apis mellifera (honey bee)

So much depends
upon the long-

bodied queen, her mandible jaws
and sharp, cutting teeth

and the two thousand eggs
that fall daily from her abdomen—

there are the large, doomed cells
of the toothless drones, fatherless

and growing, the hexagonal
brood cells crammed

with working girls who haunt
her dreams with their pollen baskets

and wax-secreting glands,
their honey sacs and double wings

on which so much depends
and we depend so much.

After weeks of nursing
and guarding, building

and cleaning those field-girl
worker bees are in the sun

and flying hard, rolled in the pollen
of four thousand flowers

that must be tapped
for a single spoon of honey.

One worker girl is dancing
the waggle dance

that lets her sisters know
the latitude and longitude

of this exact field and complex
nectar patch of summer.

The ancient Greeks believed bees
were born from animal corpses

*and when Aristæus sacrificed four bulls
and four heifers, from their entrails*

*new swarms suddenly appeared
floating heavenward* like Bhramari Devi,

Hindu goddess of the bees,
who resides in the heart chakra

and emits a buzzing sound.
Pliny says bees settled on the mouth

of Plato as a child, and *announced
the loveliness of his enchanting soul*

and the loveliness too of the clover
in bloom, of the hive

full and raging—keeping the mouth
abuzz and giving up the sting.

Interruption

Gibbon Glade, PA

No one can resist the long, elegant glide
as they kettle the thermals to the high, thin altitudes.
And just yesterday, driving back from Uniontown
I interrupted their feasting and braked hard
as a single flap swooped them from tarmac
to windshield height so I could observe, up close,
that black and tawny wingspan. We dread
the distinctive *V* of flight, the two-toned underpattern
of their underwings, especially the featherless head,
prematurely grizzled the stomach-clenching red
of calamity. But the turkey buzzard is no killer
with her chicken-claws and worried eye,
and has no song, just grunts, and a gutful of immunity
to stave off cholera, even anthrax. Romantic too
when they go courting: one bird gives up all resistance
and flaps after the other, gliding and swooping
in follow-flight, twisting and turning, over and over.

Damage Assessment

Bingen, WA

Sudden ears and rangy gray-brown galloping limbs abruptly lit up by headlights. I braked quickly, panicked, and let out a bark, *Shit* or *Oh my god* or maybe *Fuck, fuck, fuck*. I was driving the speed limit for once, but my prayer—*only one please, only one*—was not answered. There's never only one and the doe came right on the young buck's hoof heels, hastening, darting, and fleet, running fast but not fast enough.

The sound was not as loud as you'd imagine, though it made me feel sick.

Outside, the night was darker than dark, blackened by months of isolation, of too-muchness, of not enough. The blankness of grief with no tools for grieving. No streetlamps. Just depleted or unlit businesses that stood back from the highway in middle-of-nowhere Bingen, Washington.

How many times had a family or breeding pair wandered onto the tar-and-chip roads that unwind down and around our metal-roofed cabin with its screened-in porch among the trees, with the White Salmon marking the edge of our world, with the starlings and house sparrows that nest every year in the eaves? I always braked in time, and into the dusk or nearly night, the deer sped off, white tails flashing, fading among the bare trees and I breathed out again, feeling lucky.

I guess it's always like that, happening so fast, too fast, and the sound of it, the sound of her, which was almost soft, a dull thud.

We pulled over to stop my hands shaking and stood by the side of the road trying to assess the damage by the flashlight's dull beam. John went to retrieve the silver headlight rim from the middle of the road, and I tried not to hear the other sounds in the night, intermittent but close by.

Most people think a group of deer together are a herd, but you could also call them a bunch, a mob, a parcel, or a rangale.

I would like to call them a rangale, but there were only two.

John was already having a bad few months, more really than a few. First his mom. Then lockdown. Then the mad dash across the country to get away from the close quarters of the city to the remoteness of the Gifford Pinchot range. Then the fires. The smoke and ash of it. The months of beloved faces on screens, there but not there, the anguish and relief of clicking *leave meeting*. Then a dental procedure and crazy TMJ—lockjaw for real—and John not able to eat anything but smoothies. Strawberry mango. Blueberry peach. Spinach and apple. Then the plane to LA and the man in 36 C who got a three-hundred-dollar citation for not wearing a mask. Then John's dad. Then the dog. Then the cat he never liked very much, but still. Then this.

The sky was overcast, no stars to steer by—no moon in her shroud.

Though an estimated one and a half million deer-vehicle collisions (DVCs) happen every year, though deer populations have doubled and many consider them to be vermin, pests, and thugs, I told myself she made it to the other side. Maybe she was limping a little, maybe her front shoulder felt bruised, maybe that knee would never be right and she would never leap a garden fence again, but she was lucky, her sister was with her, I told myself, taking care, watching out, helping her along.

We'd both been bursting into tears and sobbing hard for minutes at a time out of nowhere and apropos of nothing. Or bingeing *Succession* with silent steady tears wetting our faces.

Surely the cat was the worst thing, the last straw in a string of undoings. The blood in the second-floor bathroom where the litter box lived. Dale hiding at the back of the bedroom closet, looking stunned: the specific indelible odor of blood and cat shit, the skin and bones of him.

When I called Nationwide, the insurance adjuster wanted to know if there were any witnesses.

The rustling-thrashing in the tall weeds or bushes was worse. Much worse. *What's that?* I asked, but John wouldn't look at me, for there was nothing anyone could do to put us out of our misery.

Grusamericana (whooping crane)

Marked by Apollo with a red coin on the forehead,
this one waits, alone, solitary, unpaired

on thick extraordinary legs, not gull-like
or chicken-like, not tree-clinging or perching.

Plate II in my *Audubon* guide also shows
the acid-yellow eye, painted alert, the hint

of black feather beneath white plumage:
that black wing-tip flag flown only

to conjure fear or desire, or to flap out
and up and up in needful migratory ride.

*

At six, Ramakrishna fainted with rapture
at the sight as ancient as the Pleistocene, their heyday,

when the longed-for whooper call sounded across
wetlands that stretched from California

to New Jersey, bugle cry that begins and builds
within the twisting loops and coils of the long

esophagus. Did the fifteen birds
that were left in 1941 dream

a wet return to the marsh grass and sand
flats of the Blackjack Peninsula, or of flying

over lands with mutual wing easing
their flight as in *Paradise Lost*?

*

But what is to be done: leap high in the air,
to make a half-turn before landing?

Toss back the head, then bend a willow
neck, bowing low and throwing sticks?

Here is a philosophy of wariness
that sleeps while standing on one leg

and if I crane my neck, or use a crane
to lift my sorrow, or fold one thousand paper

cranes with hope, will I stop the radiating
sickness, bring good luck and good fortune

to the already vanished? When he astonishes
the air, bounding up and over her arched

preening shape, his crest red, his plumage
full, will she bow and dance in answer?

*

So long-legged, long-billed, and long-
lived, we imagine their love to be truer

than ours. Mated for life, both father and mother
are egg warmers and heeders, though out of two

eggs only one survives, and sometimes I
miss the *ker-lee-oo* and rusty mottled

feathers of my sister—full of the sadness
discernable in the salt marshes, that arises, perhaps

from their having once harbored
that trumpet blast and dancing whooper logic.

Cento: My 1970s Second Wave

Off our backs, what is a woman?
This sex which is not one? A monologue?
The first estate? I am what I am

if that's all there is: a vagina on trial,
the female man, a feminist tarot,
a Jane song and bitch manifesto,

visual pleasure and narrative cinema
after the death of God the father when God
is a woman and women talk back.

When we dead awaken, let's put porn
back in the closet with the laugh of the Medusa,
the traffic in women, and the simple story

of a lesbian girlhood. Reaching beyond
intellect, you are what you eat: the female
eunuch, mom on a hook, soldiers

in the street, half of China. For we
have had abortions against our will
in search of our mother's gardens

and after the lies, secrets, and silence,
I wanted a wife. I wanted to pick your brain,
de-sexing the language toward a philosophy

of women's liberation happening in our minds
like the coming of Lillith—and tell me, why
have there been no great women artists?

The Wondrous Transformation

(six plates from Maria Sibylla Merian's
Metamorphosis Insectorum Surinamensium, 1705)

Now I am ready to tell how bodies are changed
Into other bodies – Ovid

I.

She called them worms. She praised
their lowly life and found connections
to her own. *They first come forth*
of their eggs, small, hardly
perceivable. Then they feed
properly, mandibles grinding
feelers alert, and some in a few weeks,
others taking months, arrive
at full growth. *Some are barbed.*
Some have two whirring feet
on the last hinged joint.
Some have four feet and when
they creep along their fore
and hinder meet (*these are called loopers*)
though the magus has no feet
and slides on its abdomen
like a snake in a desert
on the other side of time.

There were maggots that changed
into small brown worms
caterpillars that emerged
from their tangled shrouds as flies.
All sorts change their skins

two or three times before spinning
into webs and like silk worms
are pinned to terrestrial life by a thread:
their heads hang downwards
and in plate 63 they look serene—
you can almost hear them keening
like the bowhead whale
or other unfettered beings.

In two or three weeks proceed
night moths, the summer birds.
No more jaws or mandible, no mouths,
no hunger. No more mercurial
crawl toward a leaf or a stem. Slender
but not starving, they suck food
through the long thin spines
between their eyes. There will be
no more transformations.
They remain in this winged form,
(she had seen it happen over
and over) until they lay their eggs and die.

2. Plate 9, *Granaat boom* (pomegranate)

When adultery was a crime that could only
be committed by women, and guild rules
banned her from painting with oils,
she mastered the art of grinding pigment
into light—smooth enough to dissolve
in water and load a fine sable brush.

She went to Suriname to seek for herself
the marvelous sheen of the Morpho,

whose iridescent wings flash azure
but when viewed through a magnifying glass
appear *as minute, overlapping pantiles*
on a roof in Amsterdam.

Her detractors insist the other creatures
in this ecology of *Punica granatum* are a fantasy:
The swallowtail's discarded pupa
would not attach here on the pomegranate tree
and that hawk-moth caterpillar with eight
blind eyes dotting its ochre side
feeds on gooseberry and fuchsia.

History records her exacting patience—
her gift for transmuting what the eye sees
into spiracle and setae, filigree of hieroglyph
on open wings—and teaches her love of jewel tones—
ultramarine from crushed beads of lapis lazuli
for the blue Morpho's wing, deep vermilion
ground from cochineal worms quickens the pulse
and fills the pomegranate's seeds with blood.

The *Studienbuch* and eighteen collected letters
detail the curious plants and critters, dates, places,
amounts, and times, and her astonishment
that within the stilled *date kernel of the pupa*
was life nevertheless but nothing of the hungers
painted here: on almost every red-veined leaf,
the caterpillar chews hole after jagged hole.

The gorgeous broken open fruit makes me think
of Ovid's Proserpina swallowing the slick
pulp of seven glassy seeds, meat that keeps her

prisoner of the flesh, betrays her need
and crowns her queen of the underworld.

3. Plates 16 and 33 *Chaschou boom* (cashew) and *Vygen* (fig)

If she was patient, and could abide
the sometimes putrid smells
and sights, she could use the word *miraculous*
to divine their transmutation
and render in paint, all at once,
each tedious stage of the procession
from egg to worm, pupa to moth.
In plates like this one, Merian
defied the conventional wisdom
of spontaneous generation,
pairing each larval summer bird
with a plant on which she'd seen it feed.

In the fashionable rage for pinning
and naming, for tidying worlds
into cabinets and specimen boxes,
no one cared about insects—God's castoffs
unnaturally birthed from cabbage
or meat. But she pursued the holy mess
of plant and seed, carapace and parasite,
recording habits and predilections
responses to touch or sound, their prayerful
looping forward movement.

In lieu of Dutch allegory, each plate
distills the art of attention. Just so,
the Amber Phantom's waxen eggs

mound on the hardy cashew leaf.
And just below, a hairy, white-as-snow
looper splays flat as a pancake
though it will hatch seven or eight
weeks later. A few plates later, the elaborately
patterned fig sphinx moth
hovers above a tree hosting several
different stages of the crawler: one
with yellow stripes that sheds a sky-blue skin
to spend a few weeks unhungry, still, a pupa.

Beneath her hand, the soul unfolds, spitting out
an amber thread and twisting slowly
into hazy oval sleep. Imagine attaching
the only self you know to the stem
of the delicate cashew flower and carefully
in the dark, unbecoming something else,
trading fourteen marching legs of onward
and feed for two pairs of scaled wings
a coiled proboscis and nectar.

4. Plate 57, *Gujava rubra acida* (sour guava)

Between branches, an arched cerulean
being floats nearly fluorescent. The white
fingerlike stripes that mark her hind end
are punctuated by seven ovoid dots, all pupil
like the blind, surprised eyes of cartoon characters.

Another dazzling caterpillar twists and grasps
already clamping down on the next
pinnate leaf. In her notes about the plate,
Merian writes that it thrashed a long time

when poked with a finger. A single maroon spike
emerges from the tail, harbinger of its destiny:
the ridged reddish pupa that rests one branch down.

It was Merian's way to include all the stages
of metamorphosis in each print—no need
to reach back into memory and recall
what you looked like then, how you danced
or ate with gusto, or twisted between the stems
of your favorite fruit tree.

When my mother withdrew into a kind
of hibernation, she spun a cocoon from the pastel
yarns she fashions into caps and scarves and emerged
utterly changed. I miss her, though this quieter
mother is also kind and notices things.

She looks at photos of herself leading a line of dancers
in the *lorke* or *kochari,* one hand on her hip, the pinky
of her other hand entwined with a woman
whose name she can't recall and is filled with doubt

and wonder. Even her tongue has forgotten
how to separate one word from the next,
to push against the bottom teeth
for the fricative and shift the lips from kiss
to grimace for *what, who, where,* and *when.*

Like the dull brown sphinx moth
that spreads its geometric patterned wings
in the upper corner above the flowering tree,
she went in a capable curious worm, segmented
and many legged and emerged to fly
from thistle to rose, no story to tell but of hunger.

5. Plate 17, *Amerikaanshe Kerschen* (American cherry)

The tent caterpillars
    with ultramarine skins
wore black chains

    lodged with pearls, and having
devoured the sweet leaves
    of the sweet cherry tree

devoured each another
    in July. The victor spun
an oval bright as silver

    and changed into a moth
with two meagre markings
    on its dull beige wings.

She wrote it all down
    in her notes and etched
their elaborate caterpillar markings

    in the Suriname book
but had little to say
    or paint about the Amerindians,

Warao, Caribs, or Arawaks
    (who would not be
enslaved and broken

    on the sugar cane plantations
along the river), who
    brought her strange, furred

and venomous caterpillars,
      iridescent beetles
wrapped in leaves. Did they

      bring them as offerings? Did she
pay? Was the African who earned
      a short note and her gratitude

for macheting a path
      through the impossible,
and helping her search

      for insects, not gold, a human gift
supplied by the Governor?
      She had nothing good

to say about her fellow colonialists
      and never painted or drew
the tufted grassy sugarcane,

      opportunistic and burgeoning
in yards and between
      houses. The grammia

caterpillar that can demolish
      a whole field of cane does not
appear in her book (the plants

      must have been everywhere).
But she was one of them, witness to
      the hook, the irons, burnings

and rebellions. The torn and lacerated
      leaves she and her daughters etched
onto vines and branches, the ravenous

slugs and other bloodless creatures,
pale, white or wildly colored—
        were rapacious but not cruel

like the grimacing Dutch faces
        of the overseer, face
in the window glass or mirror.

        Once the hunger stops, once
they spin or molt into
        a clean and sober pupa

or chrysalis, Merian's images
        insist, the caterpillars
renounce avarice and excess.

        Everything is redeemed
and, God's creation, they
        rise up to God on wings.

Ursus arctos horriblis (grizzly)

I.

Whether standing and surveying the distance
or foraging, fishing, digesting, or denned,
how the skinned body resembles yours: the paunch

stuffed like yours with roots and grasses,
ground-dwelling rodents, white bark pine nuts.
In the berry bushes where appetite thrives

you reach toward thorny branches and think
the sweetness before it satisfies like Western adventure
a hunting spree and carcasses left to rot

along the highways of California
where the state flag still bears witness.
In quest of the grizzly, the Cheyenne painted

their elaborate skins, performing all the rites
for making war on a neighboring nation.
Despite the uncountable near-death encounters

recorded by Lewis & Clark in their journals,
the one thousand that remain in the lower forty-eight
are almost always at least a little hungry.

2.

You have kept the mashed watch
and busted compass, bit of your own scalp
pickled in a jar, a torn and bloodstained handkerchief

for your hope chest and memory box
though nothing can staunch the foul combination:
wet dog and rotten meat, stench of hamster cage

and musky decay. The grizzly has a sense of justice
and humor, of winter coming in her muscles.
She has a den facing south and claws

that can grasp and reach articulate as fingers.
Here is a holy necklace made long before
the last Californian was shot in 1924.

3.

Don't get me wrong. Don't wander in a haze
or sing a song without purpose for she can teach
you a lesson, twist my arm, break his heart

your whole head between her jaws and then
the sudden sound of all the many bones that make a skull
unmaking as she clamps down and shakes.

Oh Grizzly, most pugnacious and ancient survivor,
on the trail, in the brush, sing loudly, ring bells
if charged, stand your ground; if attacked

make a cannonball shape, cover the back of your neck
with your forepaws. And if I am suddenly there, uncertain
of what I am or my intentions, do not look me in the eye.

What looks playful could be desperation
and in all the faces ever filmed you will discover
no kinship, no understanding, no mercy.

Washington	10-20	Idaho	est. 140	Montana	est. 460	North Dakota	1889
Oregon	1933	Utah	1923	Wyoming	est. 500	South Dakota	1890
California	1924	Arizona	1935	Colorado	1952	Nebraska	1854
New Mexico	1931	Kansas	1880	Texas	1890		

Trespass

Western Lake, WA

In secret I climbed down
to the tweaker's habitat

to the owner's absence or oblivion.
In the pea-green doublewide

a pit bull barked and whirled,
scratched and whined, trash-eating

scourge of the lakeside neighborhood—
though the lake is gone now.

The abandoned, sallow watchdog
couldn't watch me through the green

pitted door, but could he smell,
could he scent me in the wild hedges?

Is that what made him scratch
and whinny and *bark bark bark*?

Could he tell of *the branches
nobody owns*, the greenery

and brambles with their teeth?
Shiny with hunger, with greed

and without *black art* I tore through
the *blood sisterhood* and copied it down

with fingers and lips,
an intractable thief saying *nobody*

in the lane, saying *squinched* and *splurge*
and *blackberry, blackberry, blackberry.*

Later, the burrs stuck to socks and shoes
and required the painstaking pull

and dislodging of crime, of evidence
and offense, offence, and disorder.

Correctional

Graterford, PA

All of us made mistakes at sixteen, at seventeen.
We circle around. We try to own it.

Some were seduced or coerced by crack in the '80s
by heroin or cocaine.

Some were so high we don't remember
spending the night in our room talking violently
to ourselves, disturbing parents and siblings.

We can't picture or recall the dive bar
and the slammed door, or the fatally
wounded guy or who called the cops

or what happened before we woke with our head
in the closet, knife gone, gun gone, fingerprints everywhere.

Some fell from the backs of mopeds on Quaaludes,
so concussed we couldn't read those first six months inside.

Some were almost babies.

Some spent the rest of our lives trying to take back the seconds it took
with shaking hands to fashion the irredeemable.

Some still dream about the stranger every night, or the one
who ran, the one who turned on us, the one we turned on.

Some loitered in the aisles of Strawbridge's or Macy's
and walked out again onto Market Street unnoticed, skin cloaking
the Nike running shorts stuffed into our underwear.

Some betrayed our sisters and our girlfriends. Some blamed the women
in our lives. Some defended them with ardor.

Some ran from a hit and run.

Some graduated with honors.

Some had two strikes and were out.

Most will never again cross the bridge and drive
the winding tree-lined road that first took us

to the big house, its drafty gray corridors,
clanking dumbells and caged yard.

Here in the education wing we've got two hours,
and hunkered down over our desks

everyone is nodding or choked up over this poem
called "Rage" by Mary Oliver,

the tree that will never come to leaf—
the watch, dropped on the dark stones
till no one could gather the fragments—

Earlier as I hurried past the moving lines
of men toward my classroom, one CO shouted

you can't dress like that and I put my sweater on
despite the 90-degree humidity,

aware of my sweat, the heads turning in my direction, eyes taking in
the skin on my chest and neck as it turned bright pink.

Underneath my blush is skin the color of *I can leave again*
and after class, it tingles with unearned luck

as I wait in the vestibule for one side of the steel gate to slide open
and the other to slide closed.

Restorative Justice

Western Lake, WA

Sometimes a rogue wind comes to topple
    the Douglas firs that loved the easy lakefront
and never needed to drive roots
    deep into the water table. Now the lake is gone
and our dock leads only to more vetch,

more common tansy, stand after stand
    of bluejoint and foxtail, Labrador Tea
with its fragrant leaves that are both balm
    and poison. Underwater once, reservoired
by a dam that never fueled a city's nightlife,

the flood plain is a field again—with decaying
    gray scags that loll amid the scrub plants
and ruddy alders. The calm but murky waters
    that harbored pollywogs and silver carp are gone.
But the goldenrod and hairgrass have returned

in the arms of the wind or stuck to the furred
    undersides of golden retrievers and shepherds
that amble the river trail. And the river is back too,
    its white hollows and blue-green eddies.
In every salmon berry stalk and waving

cottonwood branch, there is a gust of triumph beneath
    the syntax of regret: the squaw grass
or quip-quip is at home again—its yellow-white
    unworldly bowl of inflorescence
that can be woven into a basket or ground to meal

and baked. There's yellow salsify and pearly
  everlasting that blooms mid-July.
The flowers will last until the first snow
  of winter as everything conspires
to bury us in what we couldn't see or imagine.

Dry Spell

Afterwards, I remembered some poems mistake the moment they are beginning for the end.

I remembered being among the first humans on earth to see that the end of civilization and humans and other species and of eternity will come.

I remembered Tuckerman, the first American poet to lament the destruction of our continent.

I remembered poems tipping to the right-hand side of the page because of punchy verbs, no adjectives, and nouns and verbs that force the ninth or tenth syllable to do a lot of the heavy lifting.

I remembered the quest to find what gives the line integrity.

I remembered metaphor is wish fulfillment and simile is insight, that there is a resemblance that words control and a resemblance that words cannot bear.

I took my form and meter from other animals and the natural world, which abounds in forms.

I remembered D.H. Lawrence and Muriel Rukeyser who praised the squeamish things in life.

I tried to get away from flatness.

*

I remembered poetry as a kind of singing that raises language up.

I remembered that stanza means *little room*, that form helps light and shadow move across the page.

I remembered the final syllable in a line carries power because it's the only one that doesn't have a word that follows.

I remembered the hermit thrush's pure vowels, the wolf's emotional cry of isolation, the humpback whale's jazz—that the gopher frog sings entirely out of consonants, all edge.

I remembered Williams's language becoming much more iambic when he was stirred and Stevens using iambs to produce a singing that can't be found in formal verse.

I remembered meter elevates the flaccid aspect of prose into poetry that otherwise would just be talk.

I remembered each singer has a repetitive way of speaking.

I tried to attach myself to a tradition of chant and to find an unpredictable formality—to register the rhythms of my response to experience.

I believed that free verse gives us a homemade world of our own.

I remembered praising poems that were just talk.

*

I remembered rhyme is like an inchworm that prays itself forward with inspection and faith and is given to those who believe.

I remembered circularity and the melody of vowels.

I remembered the word order we use in speech is so fixed in its rules that certain kinds of rhyme are impossible, and certain rhythms are illegal.

I remembered Dylan Thomas's worksheets always had a list of possible rhymes.

I remembered the greatest poems achieve the simultaneous production of sound and meaning without strain.

I remembered that voice brings music to a poem but the music must remain in the words after the voice has broken.

I remembered the music of poetry creates an opening of the self and giving away of the self to the other.

*

I remembered Whitman's love of bodily life and Thoreau's unhappy reserve.

I remembered a word is a sound that means.

I remembered that language must be brought out of the self like lumps of physicality.

I remembered Osip Mandelstam who is hard to translate because he was so intelligent.

I remembered Rilke and Christopher Smart, Delmore Schwartz and Berryman, Creeley and Allen Ginsberg and William Stafford who in his poem thought hard for us all.

I remembered Gwendolyn Brooks and Muriel Rukeyser and a few other women whose poems made their way into that marbled inner sanctum.

I remembered the problem with some poets' work may be that they write with the affections.

I remembered that everything that uses language is humanized.

I remembered Paul Celan and the names that whispered to me down the years and my own hands keeping silent.

I remembered writing with the affections.

*

I remembered the basic criteria for good poetry depends on a degree of sympathy, kinship, and respect.

I remembered that song and poetry connect us to the other creatures who also sing.

I remembered sending the poem to the next stomach like a ruminating animal until it tasted most of myself—

and to put the right noises in the right order, like any good mammal.

I remembered to make the poem unfold in consciousness.

I remembered to address myself to everybody though no one was listening.

I remembered to project emotion into time with the maximum amount of flexibility.

I remembered fatigue is what makes cowards of us all and cowardice can sometimes be mistaken for fatigue.

I remembered the marathoner who knows to pass through the 21-mile wall and go beyond it.

I remembered that even anaphora has its limitations.

And I remembered *days wandering: wondering, what, anyway, was that sticky infusion, that rank flavor of blood, that poetry, by which I lived.*

Together and Apart

Ardmore, PA

Before then became now:
conversation was a mouth
forming sounds close enough

to breathe in her ginger tea or touch
someone else's shoulder, my chair
beside the scroll that hangs

in her living room where I've
never been. It shows the *enso*,
imperfect circle of emptiness

or its opposite: the most popular *kanji*
in Japanese calligraphy, it touches
my mind and describes the beginning

and end of all things or the moon
on water like a *koan* that instructs
us not to seek doctrines, teachings

or meaning. The *enso*
can only be drawn by high
Buddhist priests who sit *zazen*

for hours before dipping
their brushes into squares
of ground ink. With a green screen

and bookshelves from the British Library
you can block out the poverty
of your day-to-day surroundings

that want to scream or break through
to the occasional and unexpected
but through a scrim

or a flickering screen it's difficult
to see the imperfection that is perfect
the serenity that spins out

over ocean and field. For now,
we set a timer and draw
a tight spiral on unlined paper

for two minutes, more or less,
trying to remember the moment
when then became now.

That's how long it takes to answer
the questions in the present tense:
Where are you? How did you get there?

What's to your left? What's behind you
or up in the air before that time before now
passed away? In the Zoom grid

everyone's head is bowed to the task
or blackened to a name. Maybe next year
we'll walk together in the rain

toward the park up the street
or dry off some benches and sit
quietly, together, not waiting.

Canis lupis (timber wolf)

With a gaze that can blind
and breath that cooks meat
you have sharpened your teeth
the better to greet
the better to see
the better to bear hug
and what-big-teeth me.

The gray rankled kin
of my own dog o' diamonds
who is three feet at the shoulder
and lithe with damp,
a mouth of eager.

She too rolls in death
and wears her drives
on her winter-thick coat
and in the chain links
that collar her neck. She still bears
your lope and fear grimace
that spooks the neighbors
like the *how how how*
against backfire and gunshot.

All growls and whinnies
she gambols in her sleep
but is afraid of the large
and hooved, the moose and elk
even the deer, the sleek timber wolves
who live on the prowl
and need no shelter, pursue.

She has bristled where the wolf star
brightens and the governor of Wyoming
says he'll be first in line to kick-start
the halving and quartering, the hanging
from fence posts to send a message
through the cowboy state
that the wolf has been
re-classified as vermin.

Deity or devil are you committing crimes
or strengthening the herd?
Our house is down.
Our straw is scattered.
And you are once again
on the run from the gunshot
and fire-breathing strangers.

In all the beginnings a wolf is always
and already, and won't we all be ferried
in the end to the other side
by wolf-eared Charon, where the wicked old
and big bad is dead, is dead, is dead.

Eclogue with Fire

Western Lake, WA

In a staid place, a grave place,
the blue startling heat turned cloudy.
We had escaped city crowding,
the maskless masses who exercised,

breathing too close by far. In the mountains
everyone complies. We hunker down
and hunker in. Voices are mute-able
if I am the host and faces mutate,

turned by a trick of the camera
to mirror some face-to-face closeness
or before-time dream. Now the horizon
drifts towards nuclear wintering, smoke

that chills—an unmoved and unmovable feast,
it speaks of orange blast, the steady roar
of burning bears and mule deer, jack rabbits
and coyotes. Even the meadow is off limits,

even breath, but the river is constant
and does not grieve, lightless, grim,
its eddies spinning bitterness and ash.

The Land of Nod

Oxnard, CA

The night after she returned from the hospital,
the uneven rumbly liquid breathing of one soon

to go under kept me at the surface of thoughts
I couldn't escape. Clonazepam, Lorazepam,

not even Ambien could pull or sink me. And in the morning,
sure enough, we couldn't coax or shake her awake

except for a few seconds when someone or thing
wrenched her eyes open and let her answer *no*

to every question in a scornful voice we'd never heard before,
before pulling her down to that rocky undertow.

Through the morning and afternoon every breath,
a grunt, a rattling that soaked the bedclothes and pillows in sweat.

Then at 3 p.m., she returned—recognizing her two daughters
speaking her own name and the name of the president.

The hospice nurse put a line through the word "Comatose"
scrawled at the top of her chart and for the next few hours

a light or absence seemed to emanate from her almost
emptied irises. No sentences. No speech as the white

nimbus of hair, thick and lively around her head
nodded *yes* to sitting up and getting dressed—

to sweet potatoes and *Jeopardy!* as though part of her
remained in that rheumy underwater place

that took her breath away and wiped out the syntax
of explanation and inquiry, leaving only

no I won't and *certainly not* and *don't ever wake me up again.*

The Air Outside

Western Lake, WA

Now the air outside
that is inside is the matter
and what's the matter—

the pathetic fallacy that coats
surfaces and certainties
glazes both the glass and window

sill, my objective correlative
for what I cannot feel
as everything extinguishes around us.

This smoke is the smoke
on the other side of inside
extending across time zones

and mountain ranges, turning
the sun earlobe pink through windowpanes
even on the eastern side of the continent.

Double quarantined, I taste the cigarettes
I gave up years ago, smoke coating
my hair and my fingertips

that reach through a kind of fog
to brush the needles and branches
of the thirsty Jeffrey pine that may be next.

NOTES & REFERENCES

"A Visitor": AQI: air quality index.

"Mean Season": Joan Didion, "Los Angeles Notebook" in *Slouching Towards Bethlehem*.

"Incilius periglenes": Tubal and Jabal are referred to in spells that use frogs in the pamphlet *A system of magick; or, a history of the black art: Being an historical account of mankind's most early dealing with the Devil; and how the acquaintance on both sides first begun*, by Daniel Defoe.

"All Day": "All day" is a life sentence. "All day and a night" is life without parole. Most of the italicized words in this poem are from Allen Ginsberg, "Howl," in *Howl and Other Poems*. Statements in quotation marks are from various poems by the students from my 2019 poetry course at SCI Phoenix, Graterford, PA.

"Trichechus manatus": Georg Steller, *Journal of a Voyage with Bering, 1741–1742*.

"At the Glen Canyon Recreation Area": *Operation Glen Canyon*, informational film produced by the United States Department of Interior, Bureau of Reclamation, 1983.

"Rigging Day": J. Thomas Lamont, MD, *C. Diff in 30 Minutes: A Guide to Clostridium Difficile for Patients & Families*.

"Field Notes on the Toroweap Formation": Toroweap is a Paiute term that means "dry or barren valley." This volcanic rock is older than the rock that precedes it along the Colorado river. It appears about one-third of the way down on a sixteen-day river trip through the Grand Canyon.

"Megaptera novaeangliae": "Muxin and skrimshander" from Herman Melville, *Moby Dick*. Handicrafts practiced by sailors during long whaling and other voyages, carvings on bone, ivory, shells, and the like.

"Chelonia mydas": Christopher Columbus, *The Four Voyages: Being His Own Log-Book, Letters and Dispatches with Connecting Narratives*, edited by J.M. Cohen.

"Path of Totality": The shadow zone where it is possible to observe the phenomenon of a complete eclipse of the sun.

"Apis mellifera": Pliny the Elder, *Natural History*.

"Ursos arctos horriblis": Merriweather Lewis and William Clark, *The Journals of Lewis and Clark, 1804–1806*, edited by Bernard Devoto.

"The Wondrous Transformation": Maria Sibylla Merian, *Metamorphosis Insecto-rum Surinamensium*; Kim Todd, *Chrysalis: Maria Sibylla Merian and the Secrets of Metamorphosis*.

"Restorative Justice": On October 26, 2011, state engineers dynamited the 125-foot-tall Conduit Dam on the White Salmon River in Washington, effectively draining North Western Lake, which had been part of a lake-side community for one hundred years.

"Trespass": Galway Kinnell, "Blackberry Eating"; Sylvia Plath, "Blackberrying"; Robert Hass, "Mediation at Lagunitas."

"Dry Spell": After Eileen Tabios and Joe Brainard and in memory of Galway Kinnell. This poem is based on notes from Kinnell's Craft of Poetry course at New York University.

I would like to thank the editors of the following publications, podcasts, and websites where these poems, or earlier versions of them, first appeared:

Anacapa Review: "Trespass"
Askew: "*Trichechus Manatus* (manatee)"
Bangalore Review: "Finding the Center"
Denver Quarterly: "*Megaptera novaeangliae* (humpback)"
Fogged Clarity: "*Incilius periglenes* (golden toad)" (as "*Bufo periglenes* (Golden Toad)")
The Healing Muse: "Path of Totality"
Laurel Review: "Eclogue with Fire"
Louisville Review: "*Canus lupus* (timber wolf)"
New Letters: "*Ursus arctos horribilis* (grizzly)"
Ploughshares: "*Grusamericana* (whooping crane)"
Poem-a-Day, Academy of American Poets: "The Land of Nod"
Porter Gulch Review: "Correctional" and "Progressing to Headstand" (as "Expanding Horizons")
Posit: "Exploring the Edge," "Mean Season," and "Field Notes on the Toroweap Formation"
Prairie Schooner: "*Chelonia mydas* (green sea turtle)"
Red Rock Review: "Together and Apart"
Sierra Nevada Review: "Plates 16 and 33 *Chaschou boom* (cashew) and *Vygen* (fig)," (as "Chaschou Boom (cashew) and Vygen (Fig), Plates 16 and 33")
Split Rock Review: "The Air Outside" and "At the Glen Canyon National Recreation Area"
The Slowdown with Major Jackson: "Dry Spell"
Wild Roof Journal: "Plate 17, *Amerikaanshe Kerschen* (American cherry)," (as "American cherry tree, Plate 17")

"All Day," "Back to the Mat," "Breaking Down Barriers," "Establishing a Baseline," "Giving in to Gravity," "Heart Opener," and "In the Moment" were published in the anthology *Welcome to the Resistance: Poetry as Protest* (Stockton UP, 2021), edited by Ona Gritz and Taylor Savat.

"A Visitor," "Flyover Country," and "Interruption" were published under different titles in *Birds of North America* (Drawing Room Press, 2021), by Susan Hagen, Nathalie Anderson, and Lisa Sewell.

Many thanks as well to my colleagues at Villanova for their support, Jesse Schwartz and Melody Gleason for their assistance, and to the University for research funds and a sabbatical leave that allowed me to complete this manuscript. I am also indebted to Bau at Camargo Foundation, the Oak Spring Garden Foundation, and the Sitka Center for Art and Ecology for gifts of time, space, and companionship.

I also wish to express gratitude to those who read these poems at various stages, providing invaluable feedback and encouragement: Nikia Chaney, Ona Gritz, Genevieve Kaplan, Ann Keniston, Adrienne Perry, Catherine Staples, David Sullivan, and Suzanne Wise, and to Nathalie Anderson, Tsering Wangmo Dhompa, Claudia Rankine, and Elaine Terranova, who generously read versions of the manuscript and helped me give it a shape. To Christine Hiebert for the beautiful cover art. Finally, endless thanks to Elizabeth Murphy and Grid Books for brilliant editorial advice and much appreciated support.

LISA SEWELL is the author of *The Way Out*, *Name Withheld*, *Impossible Object*, and *Birds of North America*, an artist's book collaboration with Susan Hagen and Nathalie Anderson. She has edited several essay collections for Wesleyan University Press that focus on twenty-first century North American poetry and poetics, including *North American Women Poets in the 21st Century: Beyond Lyric and Language,* with Kazim Ali, and *American Poets in the 21st Century: The New Poetics,* with Claudia Rankine. She has received grants and awards from the Leeway Foundation, the National Endowment for the Arts, the Pennsylvania Council on the Arts, and the Fine Arts Work Center at Provincetown, and has held residencies at the Virginia Center for the Arts, Yaddo, the MacDowell Colony, the Tyrone Guthrie Center and the Sitka Center for Art and Ecology, among others. She lives in Philadelphia and teaches in the English Department at Villanova University.